Dental Hygienists

by Fran Hodgkins

Consultant:
Lori Gagliardi, RDA, RDH, M.Ed.
Former President
California Dental Hygienists' Association

Bridgestone Books
an imprint of Capstone Press
Mankato, Minnesota

Bridgestone Books are published by Capstone Press
151 Good Counsel Drive, P.O. Box 669, Mankato, Minnesota 56002
http://www.capstone-press.com

1/2001   J Fund 13.⁰⁰

Library of Congress Cataloging-in-Publication Data
Hodgkins, Fran, 1964–
    Dental hygienists/by Fran Hodgkins.
    p. cm.—(Community helpers)
    Includes bibliographical references (p. 24) and index.
    ISBN 0-7368-0808-6
    1. Dental hygienists—Juvenile literature. 2. Dental hygiene—Juvenile literature.
[1. Dental hygienists. 2. Teeth—Care and hygiene. 3. Occupations.] I. Title. II. Community
helpers (Mankato, Minn.)
RK60.5 .H634 2001
617.6′01—dc21

                                                     00-009716

Summary: A simple introduction to the work dental hygienists do, tools they use, necessary
    schooling, and their importance to the communities they serve.

Editorial Credits

Sarah Lynn Schuette, editor; Karen Risch, product planning editor; Heather Kindseth,
    cover designer; Heidi Schoof, photo researcher

Photo Credits

Gregg Andersen, 4, 6, 14, 18, 20
James L. Shaffer, cover, 12
Stephen Simpson/FPG International LLC, 8; Reggie Parker/FPG International LLC, 10
Visuals Unlimited/Bill Beatty, 16

Bridgestone Books thanks Dr. Keir Townsend, DDS; Meredith Enter, RDH; and the staff of
Townsend Family Dentistry in Mankato, Minnesota, for their helpful assistance with this book.

1 2 3 4 5 6 06 05 04 03 02 01

Table of Contents

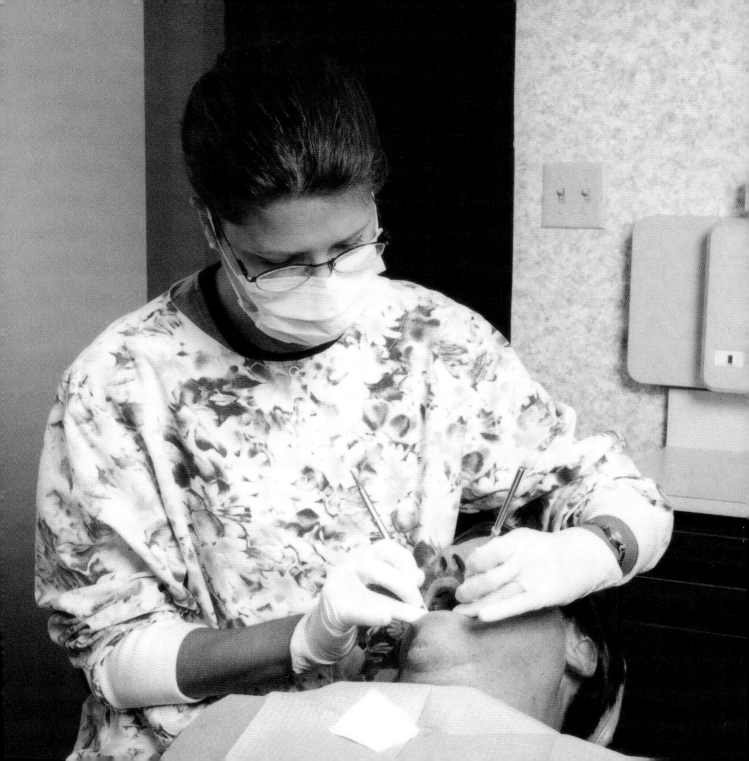

Dental Hygienists

Dental hygienists (hye-JEN-ists) examine and clean teeth. They work with dentists to treat patients. Dental hygienists teach people how to brush and floss. They help people take good care of their teeth and gums.

examine
to look closely and carefully at something

5

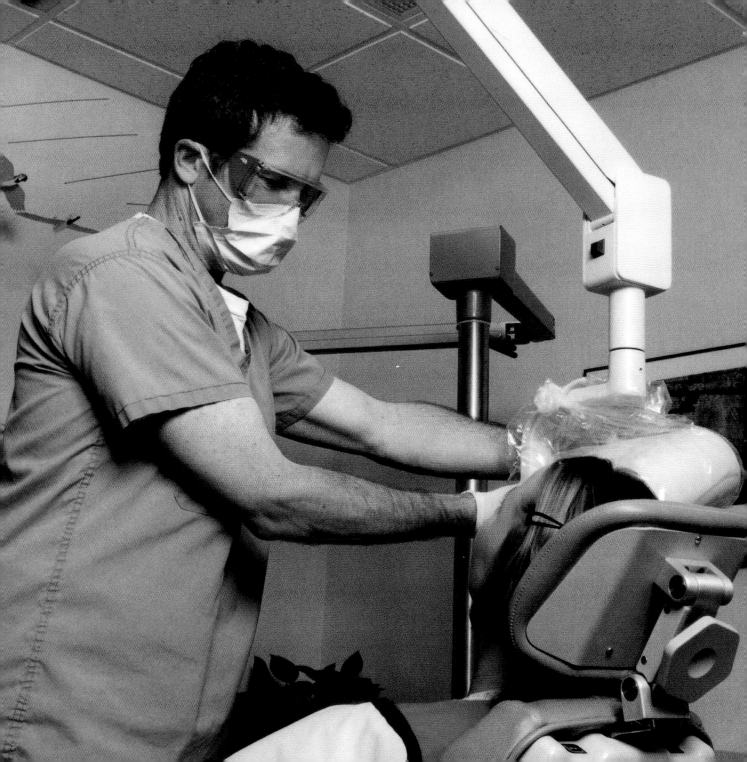

What Dental Hygienists Do

Dental hygienists examine teeth for cavities. They take x-rays. These pictures show the insides of teeth. Dental hygienists clean and polish teeth. They give fluoride treatments. Dental hygienists give toothbrushes, toothpaste, and floss to patients.

cavity
a decayed or broken down part of a tooth

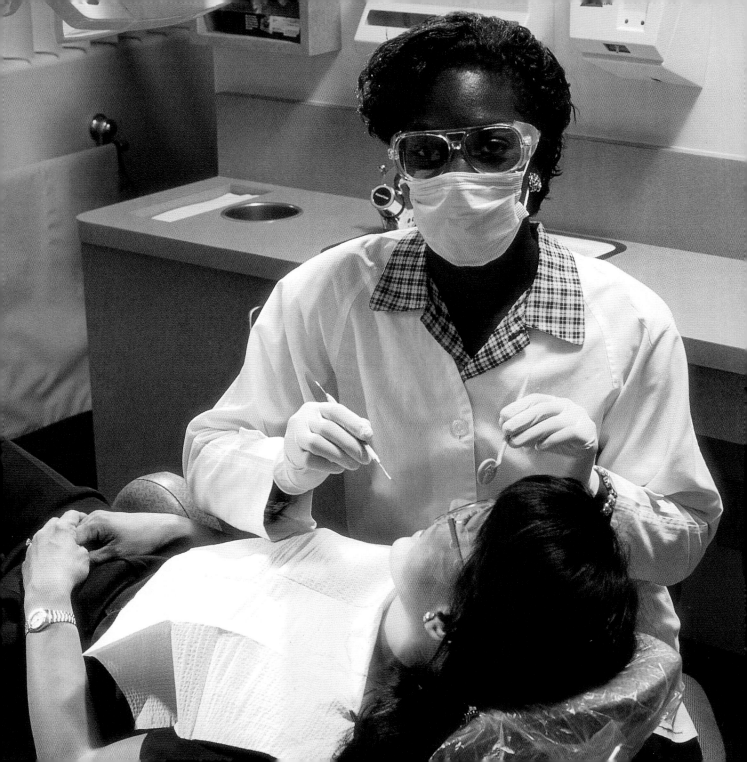

Where Dental Hygienists Work

Dental hygienists often work in dental offices. Some dental hygienists work in schools. Other dental hygienists work for public health clinics.

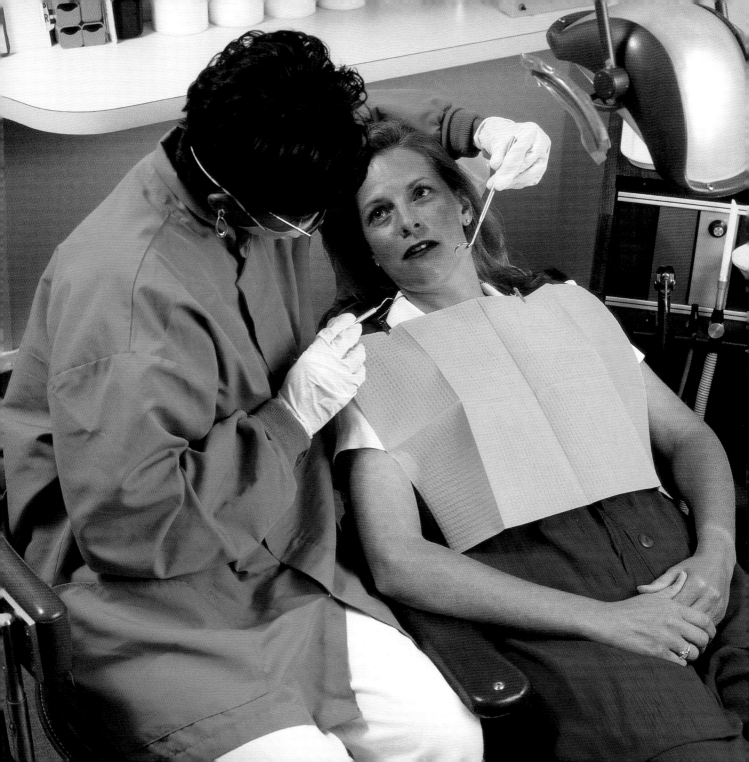

Tools Dental Hygienists Use

Dental hygienists use small mirrors to see teeth inside the mouth. They use an explorer to check teeth for cavities. Hygienists clean teeth with a scaler. Dental hygienists use a polisher to make teeth smooth. They use floss to clean in between teeth.

scaler
a metal tool that looks
like a long toothpick

11

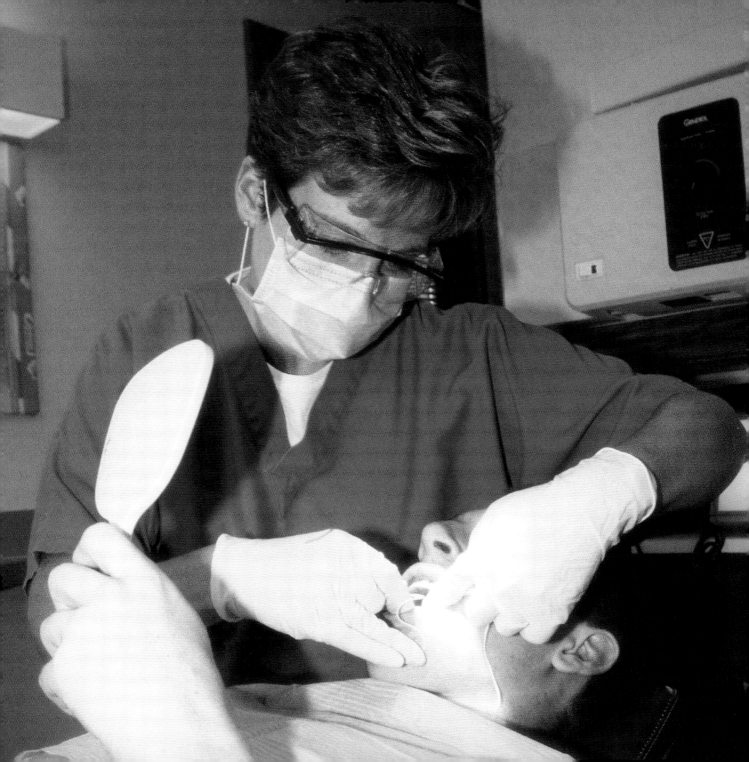

What Dental Hygienists Wear

Dental hygienists protect themselves and others from germs. They wear gloves, masks, and glasses. Dental hygienists also wear smocks or lab coats over their clothes.

smock
a long shirt worn over clothes to keep them clean

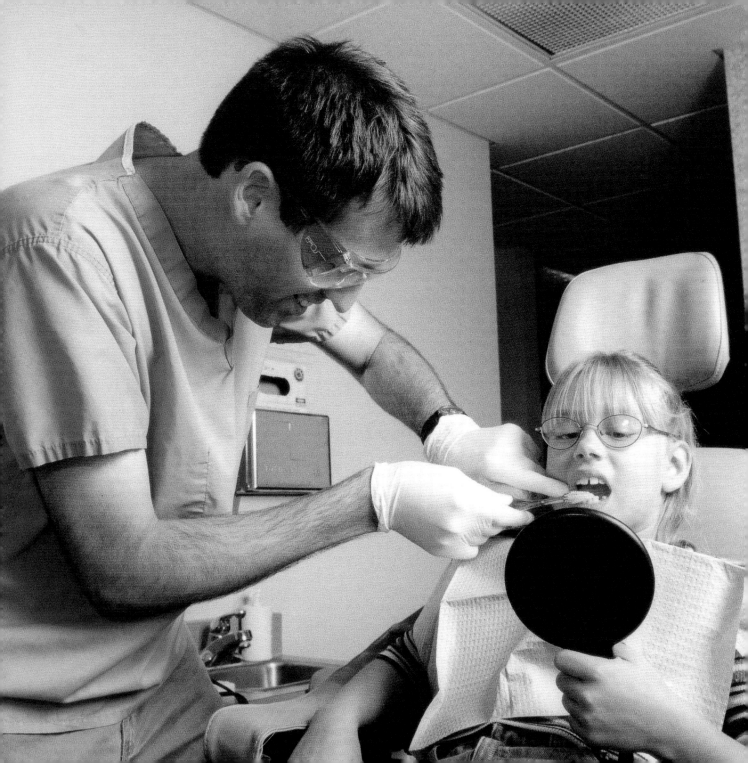

Teaching Good Oral Hygiene

Dental hygienists teach people about good oral hygiene. Some dental hygienists travel to schools. They teach children how to brush and floss correctly. Dental hygienists also tell children about snacks that help keep teeth healthy.

oral hygiene

actions taken by people to keep their mouths healthy and clean

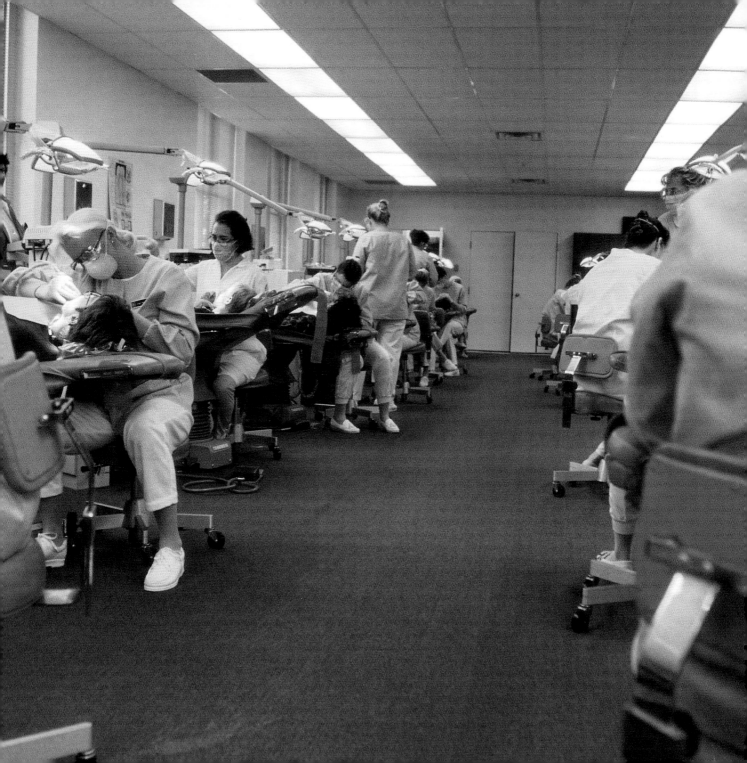

Dental Hygienists and School

People go to college to become dental hygienists. They learn about oral hygiene and take tests. Students then earn a license. This piece of paper proves that a dental hygienist has had the right training.

college
a place where students study after high school

17

People Who Help Dental Hygienists

Dental hygienists work with dentists to treat cavities and gum problems. Dentists often supervise hygienists. A receptionist makes appointments for patients. Other staff members help hygienists by setting up exam rooms.

supervise
to watch over the work of others

19

How Dental Hygienists Help Others

Dental hygienists help people keep their teeth and gums clean. They answer questions about oral hygiene. Dental hygienists teach people how to have healthy and clean smiles.

Hands On: Make Toothpaste

Dental hygienists teach people to brush their teeth with toothpaste at least three times a day. In this activity, you can make your own toothpaste.

What You Need

Small paper or plastic cup
3 teaspoons baking soda
1/4 teaspoon salt
1 drop food coloring

1 drop peppermint extract
2 teaspoons water
Spoon
Toothbrush

What You Do

1. Mix baking soda, salt, food coloring, and peppermint extract in the small cup.
2. Add 2 teaspoons of water to the mixture and stir with the spoon until the mixture forms a paste. You may add more baking soda if the paste is too thin.
3. Brush your teeth with your toothpaste. Throw the cup away after you are finished.

Toothpaste that you buy in a store has fluoride added. Fluoride helps make teeth strong and helps to prevent cavities. You should use toothpaste with fluoride to brush your teeth every day.

Words to Know

cavity (KAV-uh-tee)—a decayed or broken down part of a tooth

explorer (ek-SPLOR-ur)—a thin metal tool with hooks on the end; dental hygienists use explorers to check teeth for cavities.

floss (FLAWSS)—a thin strand of thread used to clean in between teeth

fluoride (FLAWR-ide)—a chemical put on teeth to prevent cavities; dental hygienists give fluoride treatments to patients.

gum (GUHM)—the firm, pink flesh around the base of a person's teeth

polisher (POL-ish-uhr)—a tool with a rotating tip; polishers look like electric toothbrushes.

Read More

Ready, Dee. *Dentists.* Community Helpers. Mankato, Minn.: Bridgestone Books, 1998.

Vogel, Elizabeth. *Brushing My Teeth.* Clean and Healthy All Day Long. New York: PowerKids Press, 2000.

Internet Sites

American Dental Hygienist Association—Kids Stuff
http://www.adha.org/kidstuff/index.html
Healthy Teeth
http://www.healthyteeth.org
What Does a Dental Hygienist Do?
http://www.webquarry.com/~lgfd/dental_h.htm

Index